THE *DIARY OF A WIMPY KID* SERIES

MORE *DIARY OF A WIMPY KID* BOOKS

DIARY
of a
Wimpy Kid

WRECKING BALL

BY JEFF KINNEY

THORNDIKE PRESS
A part of Gale, a Cengage Company

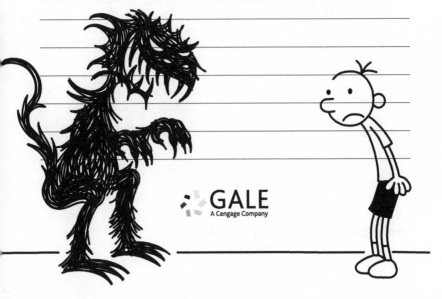

GALE
A Cengage Company

Thorndike Press, a part of Gale, a Cengage Company.

Thorndike Press® Large Print Middle Reader

The text of this Large Print edition is unabridged.

Other aspects of the book may vary from the original edition.

Set in 16 pt. Plantin.

**LIBRARY OF CONGRESS CIP DATA ON FILE.
CATALOGUING IN PUBLICATION FOR THIS BOOK
IS AVAILABLE FROM THE LIBRARY OF CONGRESS**

ISBN-13: 978-1-4328-6949-6 (hardcover alk. paper)

Published in 2019 by arrangement with Amulet Books, an imprint of Harry N. Abrams, Inc.

Printed in Mexico
Print Number: 02   Print Year: 2020

TO SCOOTER

MARCH

<u>Sunday</u>

I've read that in ancient times they used to bury kings and pharaohs with all their possessions. Back then I guess they thought you could take your things WITH you into the afterlife.

Well, if I get buried with all MY junk, I might really REGRET it later on.

Mom's having me do some spring cleaning to get rid of things I don't NEED. Well, that seemed like a good idea until I realized just how much stuff I've actually GOT.

I spent the whole morning going through my closet, and it's crazy how much was packed in there. And it's not like it was ORGANIZED or anything. I've basically been throwing things in my closet since we first moved in.

Digging through my closet was like going through my CHILDHOOD. And the farther back I went, the further back in TIME it took me.

The stuff near the front of the closet was all junk I tossed in there over the past year, like homework assignments and comic books. But after I got those things out of the way, I started finding stuff I FORGOT about.

I found a model rocket I got for my tenth birthday and a costume I wore for Halloween a few years ago. And there was a bunch of other things I didn't even know I still had.

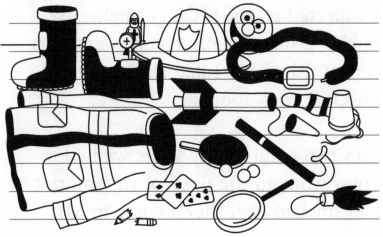

When I dug a little DEEPER, I found something I thought I'd lost YEARS ago. It was a binder full of stickers I collected in the third grade.

I used to be OBSESSED with stickers, especially the scratch-and-sniff kind. I collected all the GOOD smells, like bubble gum and cotton candy and that sort of thing, but I had all the really GROSS ones, too.

So when a kid on my street wanted to know what giraffe poop or rotten meat loaf smelled like, they'd come to ME.

One of these days I'm gonna write my AUTOBIOGRAPHY, and it's gonna include scratch-and-sniff stickers to mark all the different moments in my life.

I kept digging through my closet and found stuff from KINDERGARTEN, like a fish I made by tracing my hand on a piece of construction paper.

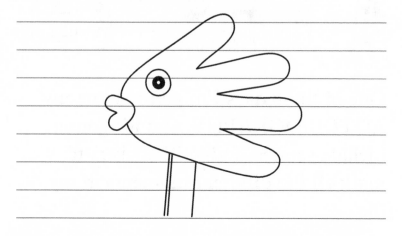

I used to LOVE doing arts and crafts back then. And if anyone ever tried to BULLY me about it, they'd get a face full of glitter.

Another project I found in my closet was a gift I made for my mom in preschool but never gave her. It was a paper flower with a picture of my face in the middle, glued to a popsicle stick.

When I made the thing, I put it in a little clay pot filled with dirt. But I tripped on the front step when I got home from school that day, and that's why I never gave it to her.

I was GLAD when I finally reached the back of my closet, but to be honest, I was a little DISAPPOINTED, too.

When I was younger I read this book about these kids who could visit a whole different WORLD by going through their closet, and I always wondered if I might be able to do the same thing with MINE.

But I thought that whoever lived on the other side might not be too happy with me for tossing all my JUNK in there over the years.

When I told Mom I was done emptying my closet today, she said I needed to put everything into three piles: one to keep, one to donate, and one to throw away. But I figured if I had to let go of any of my junk, I might as well make some MONEY off of it. So I decided to have a YARD SALE.

Mom thought that was a GREAT idea. So she gave me a magazine that had all sorts of tips for how to do it RIGHT.

All the ideas in the magazine were corny and old-fashioned, though. There was one section on how to create a sign to get people to come to your yard sale, and all the examples they showed were really BORING.

I knew that if I wanted people to actually show up at my yard sale, I needed to do something a little more EYE-CATCHING. So I whipped up a sign I knew would do the trick.

16

$100 BILL

FOUND ON SIDEWALK

PLEASE COME TO
12 SURREY STREET
TO CLAIM YOUR PROPERTY

I made a few copies of my sign and headed out to post them around the neighborhood. But Mom stopped me before I got out the front door.

Mom made me make signs that were more like the ones in the magazine, and after I was finished, I stapled them to some telephone poles on our street. Then I hauled everything down from my bedroom and started setting it all out on some plastic tables.

Each table had its own category, like "clothes" and "books" and that kind of thing. But some stuff wasn't easy to categorize, so I had to get creative.

I had a bunch of gifts from my grandparents and older relatives that I've never even TOUCHED, so I put all those things together on one table.

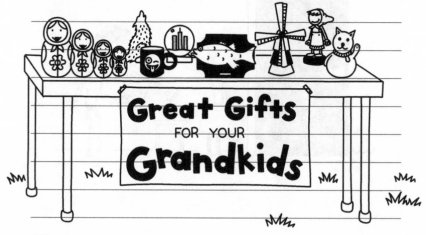

Great Gifts
FOR YOUR
Grandkids

I also had a bunch of birthday cards that were still in pretty good shape. So I used some white-out to cover my name and set them out on their own table.

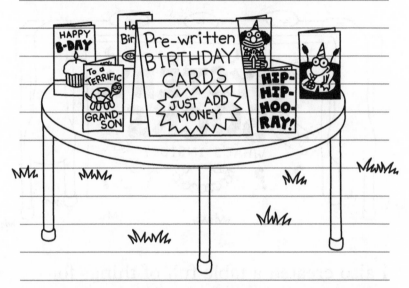

I put all my broken toys on another table and hoped some little kids who couldn't READ would come to the yard sale.

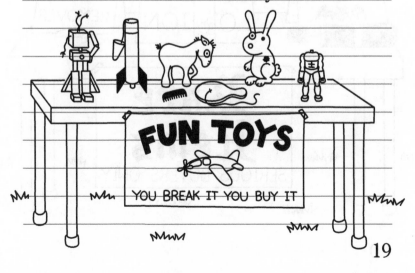

I stuffed all my random items, like marbles and a few pencil stubs, into some tube socks and thumbtacked them to a table.

I also created a table full of things for people who had money to burn.

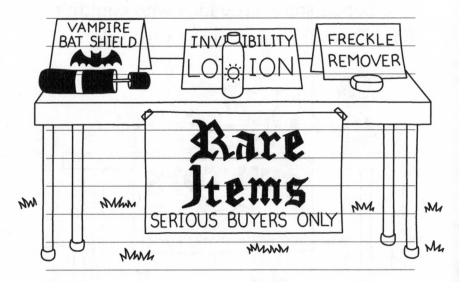

I put all my old arts-and-crafts projects on their own table, just in case some kids needed a gift for their parents but didn't want to put in the TIME.

While I was finishing up, Mom came outside to check out my yard sale, and she seemed pretty IMPRESSED. But she said I should hold on to the things I made myself, since that stuff is really SPECIAL.

I told Mom that if she wanted something, she could always buy it HERSELF. So she offered me three dollars for that paper flower I made for her in preschool.

Mom seemed pretty eager to have that thing, and I could tell it was worth more than three bucks to her. So I told Mom it was all hers for TEN.

I guess I pushed my luck, though, because she went back inside without buying ANYTHING.

While I waited for customers to show up, I started getting a little NERVOUS. I realized all my stuff was just lying out in the open, and I had no way to stop people from STEALING it.

So I called my best friend, Rowley Jefferson, and asked him to come down and be my Theft Prevention Officer.

But Rowley said he was supposed to do something with his dad this afternoon, so he couldn't help me with the yard sale.

I told him I'd promote him to Theft Prevention MANAGER, and he'd even get to wear a BADGE. Luckily, that did the trick.

As soon as Rowley got to my house, he started asking about that BADGE. All I could find was my old firefighter costume, but that seemed to make him feel important.

Rowley asked what he was supposed to DO as the Theft Prevention Manager, and I said mostly he needed to walk around and crack his knuckles to make sure nobody got any funny ideas.

But Rowley wasn't paying any attention to my instructions, because he was distracted by a table that had a bunch of birthday gifts he'd gotten me over the years.

I'm pretty sure Rowley's MOM picks out my presents, since they're always things that help you LEARN. And they're all still in mint condition, because I haven't actually OPENED any of them.

I don't know what made Rowley madder, the fact that I was SELLING this stuff or the sign I put on the table.

Rowley said I couldn't sell those things because they were GIFTS. I told him they were MINE, so I could do whatever I WANTED with them. And then we got into a big tug-of-war over the Magnet Fun set.

That's when our first customers started to arrive. I told Rowley we could argue about this LATER, but for NOW we needed to act like PROFESSIONALS.

At first just a few people showed up, but after a while a lot MORE came. And when they started checking out my stuff, I went into sales mode.

One lady seemed interested in a collector's coin I got from my uncle, but she complained that it was DENTED. So I thought fast and told her the REASON it was dented was because it stopped a bullet in World War II.

She didn't seem to BELIEVE me, though, probably because the coin was dated last year.

I spent a lot of time trying to close that deal, and I started worrying that people were stealing behind my back. Unfortunately my Theft Prevention Manager was totally useless, because he was busy playing with the magnet set.

I told Rowley he'd better start doing his JOB or he was gonna get FIRED. But Rowley said it wasn't a REAL job anyway, because he wasn't getting PAID.

I explained that I hadn't SOLD anything yet and didn't have any MONEY to pay him with. So when he said he was LEAVING, I told him he could pick out one item from any table and THAT could be his payment.

Rowley seemed pretty excited about that idea, and I thought for SURE he'd choose the magnet set. But he headed straight for the Rare Items table instead.

I explained that those things were for PAYING customers ONLY, and that maybe he'd be interested in something from the Fun Toys table. But Rowley wouldn't BUDGE.

Eventually he settled on the Vampire Bat Shield. And I was OK with that, because it was really just a broken umbrella. But now Rowley was so worried about BATS that he couldn't concentrate on his job.

While Rowley was fooling around with his stupid umbrella, I thought I saw a guy take an action figure from the Collectibles table and stuff it in his pocket. So I ran over to deal with him.

But the only things in the guy's pockets were some used tissues and car keys.

I was glad I was staying ALERT, though, because I headed off a major DISASTER. A pickup truck pulled alongside the curb, and some guy from Whirley Street started piling my stuff into the back.

I asked him what he was DOING, and he said that since tomorrow was trash day, he thought the stuff by the curb was up for grabs.

But I didn't have time to explain the concept of a yard sale to this guy, because all of a sudden I had an even BIGGER problem to deal with.

It started to RAIN, and everyone was heading back to their cars.

I was worried I might never get this many people to come to a yard sale again, and I wanted to sell SOMETHING to make all the effort worth it. So I went around and marked down the prices on every item.

Then it started REALLY raining, and I knew I was gonna have to do something DRASTIC.

I threw a bunch of stuff into BOXES, and offered even bigger discounts. But by then it was too late anyway.

I knew that if I didn't get my stuff inside, it was all gonna get RUINED. So I asked Rowley to keep his umbrella over my most valuable items while I ran everything else into the garage.

But Rowley wasn't any help at all.

He said his shift had just ended, and it was time for him to go home.

So I was on my own. I tried carrying a box of comic books into the garage, but by now the box was SOGGY, and the bottom gave out.

It took me about a hundred trips
to get everything into the garage.
But I probably shouldn't have even
BOTHERED, because most of my stuff
was already RUINED.

I figured I could still make ONE
sale, though. I told Mom that paper
flower was all hers for three bucks.
Unfortunately by then she'd changed her
mind.

<u>Wednesday</u>

I'm actually kind of GLAD nobody bought anything from my yard sale the other day, because if I ever get FAMOUS, that stuff is gonna be worth a LOT more money than I was asking for it.

I'd feel pretty dumb if I sold one of my old homework assignments for fifty cents and then someone auctioned it off later on for a few thousand dollars.

One day, they'll probably make my childhood home into one of those places schools visit on field trips.

And if THAT happens, they're gonna want to have all the authentic stuff I owned growing up.

The reason I'm not ALREADY famous is because when you're a kid, they keep you busy with school and homework, so there's not a lot of time left over to make a NAME for yourself.

But one of the ways a kid can actually get famous is by becoming a HERO. My parents watch the news every night, and there's always a story about a kid saving someone from choking or something like that.

The problem is, those kinds of opportunities don't come around that OFTEN. And believe me, I've tried to put myself in the right place for that sort of thing to happen.

But I've gotten kind of tired of WAITING, so I decided to try and create a situation where I was GUARANTEED to be a hero. I figured if I saved someone from a dog attack, they'd make a statue of me and put it in the town park, which would be pretty cool.

Rowley didn't seem so sure about my idea when I explained it to him. But when I said he'd be a part of the statue, too, he changed his tune.

So I got some bacon out of our refrigerator and had Rowley stuff it in his pockets. Then we went around the neighborhood looking for some DOGS.

We DID attract some dogs, but they weren't the kind I was LOOKING for.

Rowley got so nervous about the dogs following us that he ATE the uncooked bacon, which I've heard can be really BAD for you. So I told his parents what happened, and they took him to a doctor just to be sure.

I guess I saved Rowley's life after all, which does sort of make me a hero, if you think about it. But I don't know if that's really the kind of thing they make into a statue.

Maybe I'm thinking too SMALL with this statue idea, anyway. If I do something REALLY big, they'll make my birthday into a national holiday.

That would be pretty awesome, because then everyone will get the day off from school and work, and they'll have ME to thank for it.

The thing is, whenever there's a day off from school for a national holiday, I never even THINK about the person it's named after. I just hope that on MY holiday, people will spend the whole day reflecting on my life.

But with MY luck they'll just use it as an opportunity to sell furniture or something.

<u>Sunday</u>

All the rain we've been getting has been making everything grow like crazy. And that really stinks, because it's MY job to weed our garden.

I don't know why Mom gave me this job, because she knows I'm BAD at it. I can't tell the difference between a weed and something that's SUPPOSED to be in the garden, and I keep ripping up the wrong stuff by mistake.

I'm still not convinced there actually IS a difference between a weed and a plant. I bet there are places in the world where people think ASPARAGUS is a weed, and right now there's some kid my age busting his hump pulling it up.

I don't understand why GRASS isn't considered a weed, because it sure looks like one to ME. But people like my dad spend their entire weekends trying to get their lawn to look just right so they can impress their neighbors.

I'll tell you this: When I get a place of my OWN, I'm gonna PAVE the whole yard. That way I can spend my weekends ENJOYING myself.

I'm gonna save a TON of money by paving the yard. My dad spends a FORTUNE on lawn fertilizer, and I don't think that stuff's GOOD for you. And the proof is my neighbor Fregley, who's always out in his yard right after they spray.

I'm pretty sure all those lawn chemicals can mess with your GENES. So if I end up with a third eye or something, I'm gonna blame my PARENTS.

When I have my own place,
EVERYTHING'S gonna be different.
And I'm not just talking about the
LAWN, either.

I USED to think I wanted to live in a
big mansion with a giant gate around
it. But then I realized if I was famous,
everyone would know where I LIVED.

So my NEW plan is to build a really SMALL house that doesn't attract a lot of attention. And then all the GOOD stuff will be UNDERGROUND.

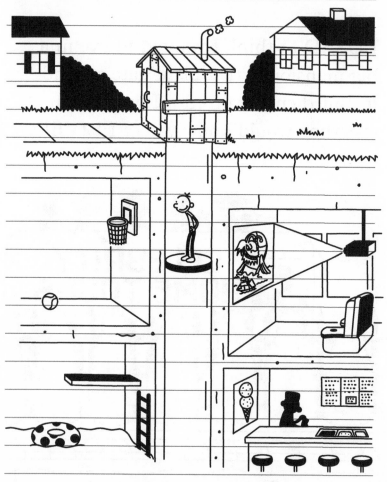

I've got ideas for what's gonna go on each level. In fact, I just finished designing the fifth floor last week, and it's probably my FAVORITE.

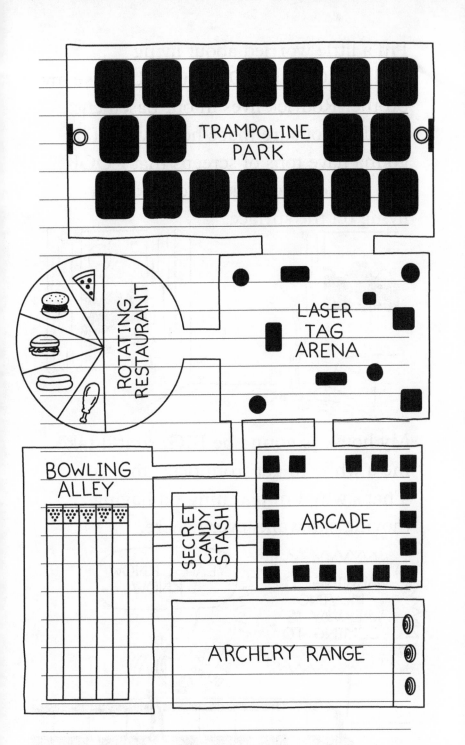

I'm a little worried about living UNDERGROUND, though, because my brother Rodrick lives in our basement, and I'm not sure that's healthy. So I'm gonna have tons of screens that LOOK like windows to make it feel like I'm living on the surface.

My house is gonna be BIG, so it'll take me a while to get from place to place. That's why I'm planning on having moving sidewalks everywhere.

My bathtub is gonna be made of glass, and it'll sit inside a giant aquarium so I can feel like I'm in the OCEAN.

My security system is gonna be SUPER high tech. I've designed all sorts of booby traps for anyone who tries to get inside.

And if someone gets past the front door, I'll just wait them out in my panic room, which is gonna have steel walls that are three feet thick.

Every so often I'll probably have a party or something so people can see how awesome my house is. But if they stay too LATE, I'll have a way to get them out of there and back up to street level.

All this stuff is gonna be EXPENSIVE, so it's going to take a while for me to save enough money to make it happen. But I figure it can't hurt to start planning NOW.

<u>Friday</u>

I was doing my homework last night when Dad called me downstairs. Mom was at the kitchen table, and she seemed pretty upset.

Dad told us Great Aunt Reba passed away in her sleep. I have a LOT of great aunts, though, and at first I couldn't remember which one she was.

Mom reminded me that Aunt Reba was the one who used to send me angry letters when I forgot to write her thank-you notes for my birthday money. And then I knew EXACTLY which one she was.

I guess MANNY remembered Aunt Reba, because he seemed pretty upset she had died.

So tonight Mom read him a book she read to ME when Meemaw passed away.

Mom has a whole SHELF of these Preston Platypus books, and each one covers a different topic. She'd pull one out every time I'd have to deal with something NEW.

When I found the books in Mom's closet, I read them all in one afternoon. I probably shouldn't have done that, though, because those books turned me into a nervous WRECK.

One of the books was about how Preston Platypus was sad that a tree in his yard died and had to be cut down. Well, when my parents said they needed to take down a dead tree in OUR yard, I was a total mess.

So my parents decided NOT to chop it down. But then a few weeks later the tree fell in a windstorm and took out half our deck.

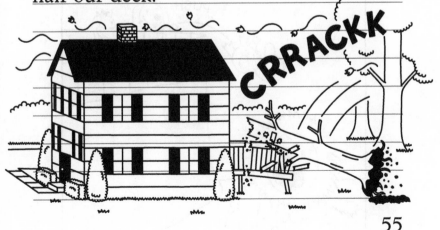

CRRACKK

The Preston Platypus books all follow the same basic formula. At first, Preston's worried about something, and then his mom tells him things are gonna be OK, and she turns out to be RIGHT.

I guess the reason I kept reading those books was because I always hoped there would be a big TWIST at the end. And then I'd be disappointed when there WASN'T.

So I started coming up with my OWN endings to the books. And when Mom saw what I drew in the back of "Preston Platypus Goes to the Zoo," she took me to see a counselor.

<u>Saturday</u>
Today was Aunt Reba's funeral. Mom said we had to go because Aunt Reba didn't have much family, so we needed to show our support.

She told us we all had to wear BLACK to the funeral, but when Rodrick came out wearing the outfit he wore to his last rock concert, Mom made him go back inside and CHANGE.

That's why we were fifteen minutes late to the funeral. When we got there, the service had already started, so we just stood in the back behind a crowd of people. I'd never been in a cemetery for that LONG before, so I felt a little NERVOUS.

That's because Rodrick always says that when you go by a cemetery, you need to hold your breath so you don't swallow a GHOST. Well, I held my breath for as long as I COULD today, but there was no WAY I could make it through the whole funeral.

I just hope I didn't swallow any ghosts, because middle school is hard ENOUGH without being possessed by a person from the 1600s.

Some of the tombstones had quotes on them, and that got me thinking about what I want written on MINE. Hopefully I'll say something really WISE right before I die, and they'll carve my last words onto my tombstone.

But I'll probably say something really DUMB, and they'll use it anyway.

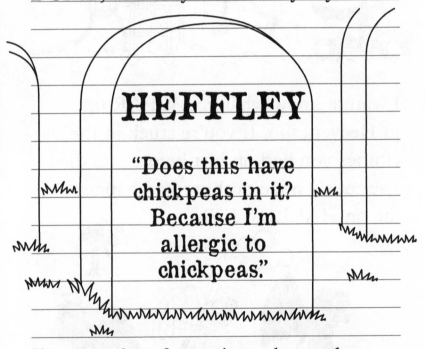

HEFFLEY

"Does this have chickpeas in it? Because I'm allergic to chickpeas."

I've got a lot of questions about what happens to you after you die. For one thing, I wanna know how you LOOK in the afterlife.

If everyone's appearance is frozen when they pass away, then Heaven probably looks a lot like Leisure Towers.

I wanna know what you WEAR up in Heaven, too. If you're stuck in the clothes you had on just before you died, I seriously hope nothing bad happens to me on HALLOWEEN.

I'll tell you this: I wanna stay alive for as long as I can. But I wouldn't want to live FOREVER.

Whenever you see a movie about someone who becomes IMMORTAL, there's always a CATCH that totally ruins it.

THE GOOD NEWS IS, YOU'RE GONNA LIVE FOREVER!

GREAT!

THE BAD NEWS IS, YOU'RE A VAMPIRE AND YOU HAVE TO DRINK PEOPLE'S BLOOD TO SURVIVE.

DANG IT!

PLUS YOU CAN'T GO OUTSIDE IN DAYLIGHT.

When a person is immortal, they always have to HIDE it from everyone else. I guess if people know you can't die, they treat you like a MONSTER or something.

But if I was immortal, I wouldn't even TRY to hide it. In fact, I'd mention it every chance I COULD.

MAKE SURE YOU FASTEN YOUR SEAT BELT!

YEAH, WELL, I CAN'T DIE, SO WHATEVER!

In school we learned about the world's religions and how everyone believes different things. In some places, they believe that when you die, you get reborn as someone ELSE.

Some people think you can come back as a totally different creature, like an animal or an insect or something. And WHAT you come back as depends on if you were GOOD or BAD.

Well, that actually makes me a little worried, because I've done a few things in my life I'm not that proud of.

And if PLANTS have feelings, then I could REALLY be in trouble.

Hopefully there's still enough time for me to make things right. Because I seriously don't want to come back as a dung beetle in my next life.

Mom told us Aunt Reba didn't have a lot of family, but she did have lots of FRIENDS, which would explain why there were so many people at her funeral.

Well, I'd better start adding some new friends MYSELF, or I'm not gonna draw much of a crowd when it's all over for me.

When the service ended today, everyone started to leave. I thought I'd recognize SOME people, because I know that Aunt Reba had a couple of sisters who are still alive. But I didn't see ANYBODY I knew, which was weird.

Mom seemed confused, too. When the crowd thinned out, we made our way to the gravesite. And that's when we figured out we'd been at the WRONG FUNERAL.

By the time we got to Aunt Reba's grave, the ceremony was over and everyone was already gone.

All I can say is, I hope Aunt Reba was looking down from Heaven and having a good laugh about us missing her funeral. But from what I remember about her, she wasn't really the type of person to have a good laugh about ANYTHING.

<u>Monday</u>

During dinner tonight, Mom said we needed to have a family meeting. And family meetings are never much FUN.

Mom told us Aunt Reba lived a really humble life in a small apartment, but that she had been careful with her money and made some really smart investments. Well, I had NO idea why Mom was telling us all this.

But then came the big news. Mom said that Aunt Reba left all her money to her FAMILY. And it took me a second to realize that included US.

Apparently, when you find out this sort of news you're not supposed to act HAPPY about it, because I guess that's disrespectful to the person who passed away. But nobody told us KIDS that.

After Mom got us to settle down, she said we needed to have a serious discussion about what to do with our INHERITANCE.

I already knew EXACTLY how I was gonna spend MY share.

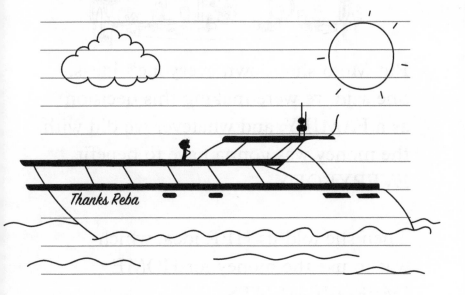

Thanks Reba

Rodrick said he wanted to use HIS share to buy a tour bus for his band, and Dad wanted to buy some really expensive figurines for his Civil War diorama. Manny wanted to use HIS money to fill up his bedroom with chocolate pudding for some reason.

But Mom shot down everyone's ideas. She said we were making this decision as a FAMILY, and whatever we did with the money was gonna have to benefit EVERYBODY.

Then she told us HER idea, which was to use the money for HOME IMPROVEMENTS.

Everyone else thought that was a really BORING idea, but not ME. I ran upstairs to get the blueprints for my dream house, and I went through them, floor by floor.

But Mom said the money Aunt Reba left us wouldn't even pay for the ice-skating rink I designed for the second level. So I tried out some of my LESS expensive ideas, like the couch with a built-in toilet.

Mom wasn't crazy about THOSE ideas, either. She said she was thinking about using the money for an ADDITION. Well, that sounded like a GREAT idea to ME. I figured if we added two more stories to the top of our house, then everyone in the family could have their own FLOOR.

Rodrick wanted to make the addition into a recording studio, and Dad wanted to make it all glass so he could show off his Civil War diorama to the neighbors.

Manny had his OWN idea for what to put in the addition, but I think it was mostly just the chocolate pudding thing again.

Of course Mom didn't like any of OUR ideas, and she said she had a totally DIFFERENT plan for what the addition should be.

Mom said she's always wanted a bigger KITCHEN, and she was really excited to use the money for THAT.

None of us really liked that idea, though, and we kept brainstorming OTHER things we could put in there.

But now Mom was MAD. She said she was the only person in the family who ever sent Aunt Reba a thank-you note for anything, so SHE was gonna decide how to use the money. And for some reason, that was the end of the conversation.

See, this is why leaving your relatives money is a bad idea. All it does is make everyone MISERABLE.

I'm not planning on leaving ANY money behind when I go. I'm gonna spend every last cent so there's nothing left for people to FIGHT over.

I can GUARANTEE that me and my brothers are gonna fight over whatever inheritance we get from Mom and Dad. And I'm ALREADY worried that I'm not gonna get my fair share.

That's because when I first learned to write my name, Rodrick made me sign a bunch of pieces of paper. And who KNOWS what kinds of things I agreed to back then.

Rodrick always says he's the "firstborn," so he'll get our parents' house and all their MONEY, too. But I don't think it works like that anymore.

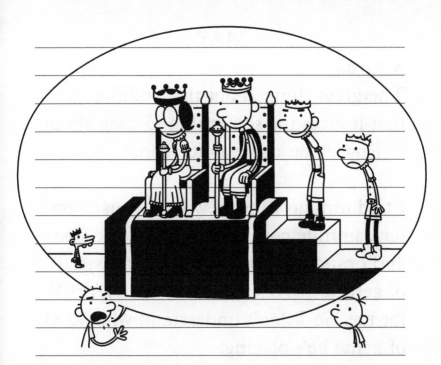

If he's RIGHT, though, then I'm glad I'm the SECOND in line and not the THIRD, because Manny's got NO chance at getting any money with two older brothers in front of him. And that's the reason I always watch my back around that kid.

<u>Saturday</u>

The great thing about this addition is that it gives me something to brag about to Rowley on our way to school.

I told him how our new kitchen is gonna have granite countertops and a tile floor and brand-new appliances. But instead of getting JEALOUS, he acted HAPPY for me. So I don't understand what kind of game he's playing.

Rowley's house is newer than ours, and it's a lot BIGGER, too.

And that's not right, because Rowley's an only child, so he doesn't even NEED all that room.

Back when Rowley first moved in, I told him we should trade houses to make things more FAIR. Rowley thought that was a good idea, but unfortunately his dad DIDN'T. And I think that's what got me and Mr. Jefferson started off on the wrong foot.

Anyway, I'm actually getting kind of EXCITED for construction to begin, because it's gonna be NICE having some more space. But I guess they've gotta do a bunch of paperwork before they can get started for real.

Dad wants to fix a few things around the house before construction begins anyway, and he wants me and Rodrick to HELP him.

Dad says once me and Rodrick get our OWN places, we're gonna have to know how to do repairs OURSELVES. I keep telling Dad that by the time we're HIS age, we won't HAVE to fix things ourselves. But he never seems to want to hear it.

Whenever Dad tries to teach me how to do something new, I always have trouble following along. A couple of weeks ago he showed me and Rodrick how to change a tire, but I guess I lost interest when he started talking about lug nuts and air pressure.

Dad was frustrated I wasn't paying attention, and he asked me what I'm gonna do if I ever get stuck by the side of the road with a flat tire. I told him I'm planning on buying a WHISTLE, and I'll just blow it if I ever need help.

I guess that was the wrong answer, though, because since then Dad's been on my case to learn how to do things for MYSELF.

Today Dad said he was gonna teach me how to "snake a drain," which didn't sound like fun to ME. And when I found out it was a PLUMBING thing, I got SCARED.

I've had a fear of plumbing ever since I was a little kid. It's all because I overheard Mom talking to Dad outside my bedroom just after we moved in.

What I didn't know THEN was that
grout is the gritty stuff between the
bathroom tiles. But when Mom said that
word, it put a picture in my mind.

THE GROUT

Since I'd never SEEN the Grout,
I figured it must hide in the pipes
whenever I walked into the bathroom.
So that made me nervous around faucets
and drains.

SLORP

I was scared that one day the Grout was gonna grab one of my ankles when I was in the shower and pull me down the drain.

And I didn't feel safe in Mom and Dad's bathroom, either, because I figured the Grout could just slither through the pipes and get me in THERE if it wanted to.

I thought maybe I could at least stop the Grout from getting out of the faucets by BLOCKING them. So one day I went around the house putting balloons over all of the nozzles, which turned out to be a pretty dumb move now that I think about it.

ZIP

BLOOSH

I knew I needed a way to DEFEND myself if the Grout ever came after me while I was using the bathroom. And I found the perfect weapon in the cabinet underneath the sink.

From then on, if I was in the bathroom, I was ARMED.

But later I started to worry that the Grout might slip out of the bathroom and get me in my BEDROOM.

And a few times I was sure it was actually right there in the room WITH me.

But when I woke up in the morning, the Grout was GONE.

BLINK
BLINK

Finally, I told Mom I was too scared to sleep alone because I was afraid of the Grout.

Mom thought the whole thing was HILARIOUS and showed me what grout REALLY was.

Then she told me that a monster is only real if you BELIEVE in it, and if I stopped thinking the Grout was real, it would DISAPPEAR.

I realized that was EXACTLY what the Grout would WANT me to think, and I wondered if the Grout was actually pretending to be MOM.

So from that point on, I kept my bedroom door LOCKED, just in case.

Eventually I guess I DID stop believing in the Grout. Well, at least until TODAY, when Dad unclogged the drain and pulled out a glob of HAIR. And for ME, that's all the proof I NEEDED.

I spent the rest of the day locked in my room. And that was where I planned on STAYING, at least until Dad took my door off the hinges with a screwdriver.

I didn't even know you could DO that. So Dad should be happy, because he actually taught me something NEW today.

<u>Sunday</u>
This morning, Dad woke me and Rodrick up early and told us we had to go with him to the home improvement store. He said he had a day of chores lined up for us, and we needed to get some supplies.

It's been a while since we went to the home improvement store, and the last time we were there, we got kicked out. That's because Manny used the toilet on the display floor.

Dad went off to find stuff to fix the washing machine, and he sent me and Rodrick to get some other things, like wood stain and paintbrushes.

I'll tell you this: If there's ever a zombie invasion or something like that, I'm heading STRAIGHT for the home improvement store. Because there's stuff in there that can do some SERIOUS damage.

When we got back home, Dad told me and Rodrick we were gonna stain the deck. He said we'd have to paint around the hot tub since it was too heavy to move.

Honestly, I wish we never GOT the hot tub, because that thing has been nothing but TROUBLE.

This winter, the hot tub almost KILLED me, not ONCE, but TWICE.

One night we had a big storm, and the strap holding down the hot tub cover came undone. So Dad told me I had to get out there and FIX it.

After I got on all my winter gear, I went outside to deal with this thing. The cover was flapping around like CRAZY, and it wasn't easy trying to wrestle it back down. And just when I thought I HAD it, a big gust of wind came and blew the cover clear off the deck.

But I was still holding on to the cover, so I went flying WITH it.

If there hadn't been three feet of SNOW on the ground, that would've been IT for me.

After I checked to make sure I didn't have any broken bones, I dragged the cover through the snow and up the stairs. And by the time I got to the TOP, I was completely EXHAUSTED.

90

But that's not the end of the story. The hose Dad used to FILL the hot tub was running down the stairs, and it was frozen SOLID. So when I STEPPED on the hose, I slid all the way back down to the BOTTOM and almost broke my neck on the landing.

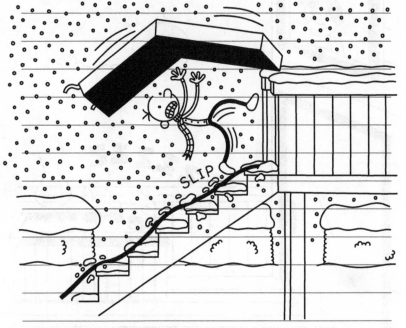

SLIP

Rodrick's had problems with the hot tub, too. He used it all winter, but had a bad habit of falling ASLEEP in it. So Mom would always have to make sure he wasn't still outside when she went to bed for the night.

But one time Mom forgot to check on Rodrick before she went to sleep, and didn't realize he was out there until the MORNING.

It took something like two WEEKS for Rodrick's skin to smooth out so he could stop looking like a PRUNE. And during that time, his high school had their yearbook photos taken.

Rodrick Heffley

A few months back, Dad drained the
hot tub, and there hasn't been any water
in it SINCE. I'm just hoping we get
RID of that thing before it causes any
SERIOUS damage.

While we were staining the deck near
the hot tub today, I heard a buzzing
noise, and thought maybe someone
accidentally left the heater running.

So I lifted the cover to check. And as soon as I DID, I knew I was in TROUBLE.

Some wasps had made a NEST underneath the cover, and now they were all stirred up. If I made a sudden move, I was gonna get STUNG. I didn't know what to DO, but Rodrick made the decision FOR me.

The wasps went BERSERK, and I dropped the hot tub cover, then RAN for it. Somehow me and Rodrick BOTH managed to get inside without getting stung.

We were really lucky, because I've read that wasps can sting you MULTIPLE times, unlike a regular honeybee, which can only sting you ONCE.

I wonder what it's like knowing that if you sting someone, you'd DIE. If I was a honeybee, I'd be tempted to use my stinger every DAY. ESPECIALLY if I was surrounded by bees my age.

But if I went through my whole life without ever using my stinger, I'm sure I'd end up REGRETTING it.

This afternoon, Dad wanted to know why me and Rodrick weren't still outside staining the back deck. Rodrick told him about the WASPS, but left out the part about spraying their nest with the hose.

Then Dad said he had another job for us in the FRONT yard. He said the gutters were clogged and needed cleaning, so we had to go get the ladder out of the garage.

Cleaning the gutters is my LEAST favorite chore, because it's always ME who has to climb up the ladder.

Dad won't do it anymore because the LAST time he did, he had a run-in with a SQUIRREL.

So now RODRICK won't go up on the ladder, either. He says the person who's the LIGHTEST has to do it, because they won't get hurt as bad if they FALL.

Rodrick even drew a diagram to show me the science behind it. And if that was supposed to make me feel BETTER, it DIDN'T.

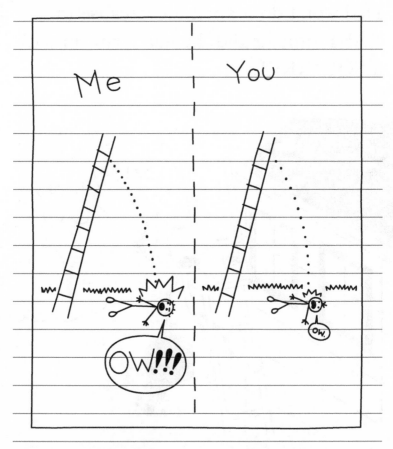

We got the ladder out of the garage and carried it to the front yard. Then we leaned it against the roof, and Rodrick held the base in place so I could climb up.

When I got to the top, I started scooping the muddy slop from the gutters into the trash bag I was holding in my other hand. That meant I couldn't really hold on to the ladder, and it was hard to keep my balance.

After I cleared out that section, I climbed back down and we moved the ladder to another spot. But on my fourth trip up, I noticed the ladder felt a little more WOBBLY than usual.

I yelled down to Rodrick to hold the ladder STEADY, but I didn't get any response. And when I looked to see if he was on his phone or something, he wasn't even THERE.

And that's when I looked through the
bathroom window and saw Rodrick
INSIDE THE HOUSE.

I knocked on the glass to get his attention.
But I must've leaned over too FAR, because
the ladder started tilting to one side.

It was too late for me to try and climb
all the way back down, so the only place
to go was UP.

I climbed to the top of the ladder and
grabbed the edge of the roof with both
hands, then pulled myself up onto it.
I did it just in time, too, because the
second I stepped off the ladder, it went
crashing to the ground.

100

So now I was stuck on the roof with
no way to get back down. I yelled out,
hoping Mom or Dad would hear me. But
I was pretty sure Dad was in the laundry
room fixing the washing machine, and I
hadn't seen Mom all morning.

Then I spotted Mr. Larocca driving
his lawn mower out of his shed,
and I thought I was SAVED. I tried
SHOUTING to him, but he couldn't
hear me over the sound of the mower.

I figured I could get Mr. Larocca's attention by throwing some of the goop from the gutters in front of his mower to get him to stop and look up.

So I scooped up some sludge and aimed for a spot in Mr. Larocca's path. But I guess I miscalculated a little, because I nailed the mower with a direct HIT.

And believe me, I couldn't make that shot again if I had a HUNDRED more tries.

SPLAP

Mr. Larocca stopped his mower and tried to figure out where the ambush CAME from. I decided maybe it wasn't so bad to be stuck on the roof AFTER all, and I scrambled to the other side where he wouldn't be able to see me.

I hid behind the chimney, which was the only shady place on the roof. And even there, it was pretty HOT.

I knew I could be in for a long wait, and after a while I started worrying about getting DEHYDRATED.

So I took off most of my clothes, because I didn't want to SWEAT too much. I thought that if I got really desperate, I might be able to wring some moisture out of my SOCKS. But I was really hoping it wouldn't come to that.

I knew that if I didn't do something to save myself, they'd eventually find me in one of those satellite photos.

It was too far to jump DOWN, so that was out of the question. And even if I landed on the back deck without killing myself, those wasps would probably finish me off.

Then I remembered there was a window on the side of the house above the garage. So I lowered myself down from the roof and onto the ledge, which was BARELY within reach.

Luckily, the window wasn't LOCKED. I opened it just wide enough for me to fit inside, and I squeezed through.

The window led to Mom and Dad's bathroom, and the ledge was right above their TOILET.

I put one foot down on top of the toilet tank, and then I tried to put my OTHER foot down on top of the LID. But I didn't notice the seat was UP until it was too LATE.

SPLOSH

So now my ankle was STUCK, and I couldn't pull my foot out, no matter how hard I tried. I guess I was making a lot of noise trying to get myself free, because that was when I found out where MOM had been all this time.

And it really wasn't fun explaining the
situation to Dad when HE came into the
bathroom.

So it wasn't a great day for me. But the
good news is, Mom said that from now
on we're getting our gutters cleaned by
PROFESSIONALS.

Tuesday

It turns out I'm not the ONLY one who got replaced by someone who actually knows what they're doing. It happened to DAD, too.

Dad took the washing machine apart but couldn't put it back together. So Mom made him hire a plumber to fix it.

@$☆*!!!

It's been really inconvenient living without a washing machine. We've had to wash our clothes by hand in the kitchen sink, which is a big pain. But Rodrick came up with a SHORTCUT last night, and put his dirty clothes in the DISHWASHER.

Well, the dishwasher did a good job WASHING the clothes, but not DRYING them.

108

And when Rodrick left the house to go to school this morning, his clothes were still WET.

So he used his van to AIR-DRY his clothes on the way to school.

Unfortunately for Rodrick, that got the attention of the POLICE, who pulled him over.

That's why Mom made Dad call someone to fix the washing machine. But I didn't know the plumber was in the house until I walked past the laundry room.

The guy must've known what he was DOING, because he got the washing machine up and running.

But things ended kind of awkwardly when Manny tried to pay the plumber using Mom's credit card.

Wednesday
When I came home from school this afternoon, there were a bunch of workers and heavy machinery in our yard.

I was super EXCITED, because
that meant this addition was finally
happening for REAL.

A guy was using a backhoe to dig the hole
for the foundation, and it was CRAZY to
see how POWERFUL that thing was.

Me and Rowley tried to dig a hole to
China once, and we quit after a few
hours. But if we could've gotten our
hands on one of THESE things, we
might've actually pulled it off.

I'm wondering if the crew would let me take the backhoe out for a SPIN. Because I could use it to pull the most epic prank EVER at my school.

It was pretty hot today, and I think Mom felt bad for the guys who were working hard. So she made some cold drinks and brought them outside.

It kind of backfired, though, because after that, the workers started coming inside to use the BATHROOM.

And when a line formed for the DOWNSTAIRS bathroom, the biggest guy on the construction crew headed UPSTAIRS to find another toilet.

And that guy was carrying a MAGAZINE, so I got the feeling he wasn't heading up there to go Number One.

I wanted to try and STOP him, so I pressed the "test" button on the smoke detector to set it off.

The workers all got out of our house pretty QUICK, but they weren't the ONLY ones who thought there was an actual emergency.

MANNY thought so, too. And when the smoke detector went off, he threw all his stuffed animals out his bedroom window, then hopped onto the pile.

Mom and Dad weren't happy with me for the smoke detector thing, but I don't think they were crazy about the workers using our bathrooms, EITHER. So this evening, Mom ordered one of those porta-potties for the work site, and now everybody's happy.

Friday

Yesterday, the construction crew poured concrete for the foundation, and today they started framing the addition. I thought it was pretty cool seeing how everything was coming together.

Unfortunately Dad noticed that I was interested in what was happening outside, and that put an IDEA in his head.

Dad said this project was a good opportunity for me to learn from REAL professionals and to pick up skills I can use down the road.

I wasn't really on board with that plan, though.

Most of those construction workers look like they've got really rough hands from working with all that heavy equipment. But I use all sorts of lotions and creams to make my hands nice and SOFT.

And I'd like to KEEP them that way, because my hands are my best feature.

But that was EXACTLY the wrong thing to tell my dad, because it earned me a one-way ticket outside.

I don't know why Dad sent ME out there and not Rodrick. Manny actually wanted to go WITH me, but Dad told him he was too YOUNG to help. And Manny didn't take it that well.

Dad told me I needed to find the person in charge and see how I could pitch in. So I asked around, and someone introduced me to the FOREMAN, who was in his trailer.

I guess the foreman was too busy to deal with some middle school kid, so he told me to go find a guy named Buddy and talk to HIM.

Well, Buddy was pretty easy to find, especially since his name was tattooed on his forehead.

Buddy was working with some guys on the framing, so I thought I'd start off by telling them who I WAS. But they weren't as impressed as I THOUGHT they should be.

I'M THE OWNER!

I told these guys I was out there to HELP them. So Buddy told me he had a REALLY important job, which was to hold up a wall they had just framed.

And I DID feel pretty important for a while, at least until I realized the wall was holding ITSELF up on its own.

Once I understood it was a prank, I figured this is just the way construction workers joke around with one another. So I picked up a hammer and asked Buddy if I could nail some boards together or something.

Buddy told me that would be GREAT, but I was holding a LEFT-handed hammer, and I needed to go find a RIGHT-handed one.

So I asked around the job site, and it took me a long time to realize THAT was a joke, too.

It hit me that since I was the youngest guy out here, the other workers didn't RESPECT me.

I figured they wanted me to QUIT, but I didn't want to give them that SATISFACTION.

I decided I was gonna PROVE myself by working hard, and move up the ranks. And maybe within a week or two I'd have guys like Buddy reporting to ME.

So I went around the construction site finding things I could do to help out. I filled some buckets with water for the workers who were mixing concrete, and I moved a pile of gravel out of the way when a truck needed to get through.

HONK
HONK

By the time we broke for lunch, I was feeling pretty GOOD about myself. But I didn't want to kick back and relax, because then these guys would think I was LAZY.

So when lunch got delivered, I went around the job site handing out everyone's orders. And that made me REALLY popular.

One guy named Luther was in the middle of mixing a batch of concrete, so I had to wait before I could hand him his meatball sub. And to be extra helpful, I unwrapped it for him so he'd be able to have it as soon as he was finished.

But I wasn't being CAREFUL, and the meatballs slid out of the sub and into a bucket of wet concrete.

Luther didn't look like the kind of guy who'd be happy about a meatball sub with no MEATBALLS in it. So I tossed the REST of the sub into the bucket and backed away.

And I'm glad I got out of there when I
DID, too. Because when Luther accused
Buddy of stealing his meatball sub,
things got UGLY.

I snuck back to the house, then locked
the door behind me. And when Dad
asked me why I wasn't still out there
WORKING, I told him I was RETIRED.

<u>Sunday</u>

Things were really moving along with the addition until our NEIGHBORS started complaining. Mr. Larocca had an issue with the NOISE, because he works the night shift at a hospital and needs to sleep during the day.

So Mom's been asking the workers to try and keep it down, but that's not easy to do when you're dealing with HAMMERS.

Our other next-door neighbor, Mrs. Tuttle, isn't happy about the addition, EITHER.

Apparently one of the workers rolled a wheelbarrow onto her property and trampled some of her flowers, and now she wants us to REPLACE them.

And it's not just our NEXT-DOOR neighbors, either. Mrs. Rutkowski lives diagonally across the street, and I guess one of her cats got into our yard and stepped on a nail. So she told Dad he had to pay the VET bill.

All this complaining is just slowing things down and making the project take LONGER. So the only person who's actually making any PROGRESS around here is MANNY.

He found a toy toolbox in the basement, and he took some scrap wood out of the dumpster. I'm not exactly sure what he's building in the backyard, but it looks pretty IMPRESSIVE.

The dumpster is definitely the best thing about this project. Whenever the trash can in my bedroom gets full, I just empty it into the dumpster, which is right outside my window.

What's even better than THAT is how easy it is now when I have to put the trash out on Sunday night. It's my job to put trash stickers on all the bags, then take everything down to the curb. And that's a giant pain, especially when it RAINS.

But with the dumpster, I don't even have to deal with the STICKERS. I can just chuck the bags straight in.

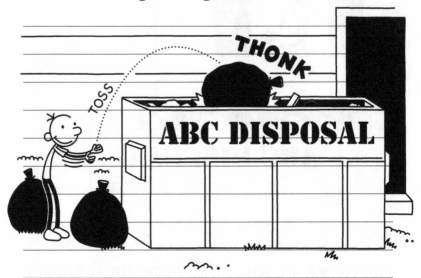

Tonight I made a pretty stupid mistake, though. I didn't feel like taking each trash bag out of the garbage can, so I tried to empty it into the dumpster all at once.

Unfortunately I didn't realize how HEAVY the trash can was, and I couldn't get it all the way over the top of the dumpster. So the whole garbage can tipped backward, and the trash emptied out of the bags.

So now there was garbage EVERYWHERE, and I had to scoop all the trash back into the bags.

To make matters WORSE, it was a windy night, so the trash was blowing EVERYWHERE. And it wasn't a lot of fun trying to chase all that stuff down in the dark.

I spent an hour picking trash out of Mr. Larocca's bushes. But I should've remembered that he works the night shift and leaves at that time.

<u>Monday</u>

<u>I got to bed super late yesterday, because</u>
<u>I had to try and convince Mr. Larocca</u>
<u>that I wasn't toilet-papering his bushes.</u>

<u>I REALLY</u> <u>wish I had gotten a good</u>
<u>night's sleep, though, because we had</u>
<u>a big test at school this morning, and I</u>
<u>don't think I did my best.</u>

This was one of those tests the whole SCHOOL has to take. The teachers have been trying to get us ready for WEEKS, because apparently the scores really MATTER.

I guess our school did really badly on this test LAST year, and if that happens AGAIN there are gonna be budget cuts. And that means some teachers could lose their JOBS.

On top of that, they might have to cut some programs, like Art and Music. I wish KIDS had a say in what to cut, because if I was the one making the calls, Phys Ed would've been on the chopping block a long TIME ago.

The teachers have been really stressed out about this test, and the last few weeks haven't been a lot of FUN.

All this pressure has been getting us KIDS stressed out, too, so last week the school brought a Stress Puppy into the library to help everyone relax. But kids got too grabby with the puppy, and then the puppy got all stressed out.

The puppy started running in circles and peeing all over the place. So the school took it away and replaced it with a Stress Lizard, and nobody wanted to TOUCH that thing.

Speaking of stress, I really wasn't looking forward to going home this afternoon, because I knew they were gonna cut a hole in the wall to connect it with the addition.

I was worried they might accidentally have to cut through the PLUMBING, and I didn't wanna be around when THAT happened.

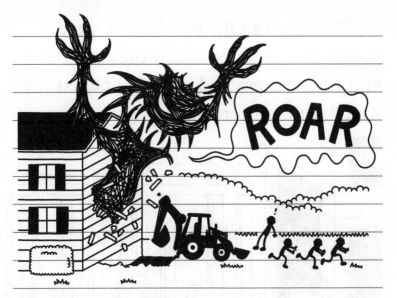

Rodrick thought they were gonna use a WRECKING BALL to smash through the wall, and his whole plan was to make a music video with his band when they DID.

So Rodrick and his bandmates were pretty disappointed when they got there and the workers had already opened the wall with a power saw.

I didn't see any sign of the Grout, so THAT was a relief. But what the workers found inside the walls was just as BAD.

The wood underneath the siding was ROTTEN, because of a leak caused by the clogged gutters. And apparently there was toxic mold in the walls, so we've been living with THAT all this time, too.

Plus, there were rodents' nests in the walls, which means we've been sharing our house with a colony of MICE.

It really creeps me out to think there's this whole WORLD living inside our walls without us even knowing it. And that's why I've decided when I build my first house, it's gonna be 100% GLASS.

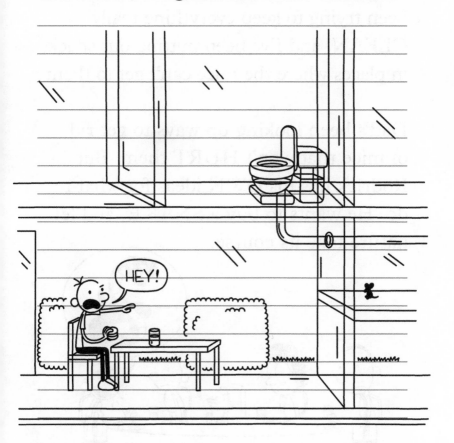

<u>Friday</u>

Ever since they opened up that wall, we've been finding mouse droppings on our kitchen counters. So that means the mice are living out in the OPEN now.

Mom says we can't leave any food lying around, because then the mice will get up on the surfaces where we EAT. So we've been trying to keep everything really CLEAN, and I've been putting our snacks in places where the mice can't get to them.

Dad's been looking up ways to get rid of mice that won't HURT them. But Rodrick has his OWN ideas for what to do. He wants to buy a SNAKE, and let nature take its course.

When Mom asked Rodrick what we'd do once the snake ate the MICE, he said we'd buy a MONGOOSE to catch the snake. So remind me not to visit RODRICK'S house when I get older.

The mice aren't our ONLY problem, though. We've got WASPS in the house now, too. Mom found one crawling on the mantel above the fireplace last night, and there was another one flying around the kitchen this morning during BREAKFAST.

BZZZZZ

We can't figure out how they're getting INSIDE, because we've been keeping the windows shut and we don't open the front door unless we HAVE to.

Mom thinks they might be coming in from underneath the tarp that's covering the side of the house, so she sent Dad out there tonight to make sure there aren't any gaps where they're getting through.

But Dad wasn't happy about it, because there was a THUNDERSTORM.

I would've HELPED him, but I was
afraid of being struck by LIGHTNING.
At school, Albert Sandy told us about
this kid who got hit by lightning while
he was out in a canoe, and now he's
SUPERCHARGED with electricity.

Well, everyone at my lunch table thought
that sounded pretty COOL, but I know
that if it happened to ME, everyone
would just use me as a charging station.

Rodrick had a theory about how the wasps were getting in, but it sounded kind of CRAZY.

He explained there are all different TYPES of wasps, like paper wasps and mud wasps. He said we've probably got SEWER wasps, and they're getting in through the TOILETS.

Well, I've never heard of a sewer wasp before, but I'm not taking any CHANCES.

Right now we've got a rodent problem and an insect problem, and I'm not sure which is WORSE. I don't know why our house can't be infested with something CUTE instead. Because if we were overrun by KOALAS, I really wouldn't have a problem with it.

146

<u>Saturday</u>
Last week the workers had to disconnect our air conditioner so they can bring in a bigger unit. So for now we're all sleeping in the basement, because that's the only place in the house where it's COOL.

I can see why Rodrick likes it down there, ESPECIALLY in the summer. I don't love being underground, though, which is making me rethink the whole plan for my dream house.

Dad said when he was growing up, some people built BUNKERS where they could go if there was a war or something.

Well, living in a tiny underground space with my whole family sounds like a TERRIBLE idea. First of all, the snacks would be gone by the second day. And if we only had one bathroom down there, we'd have MAJOR problems.

I guess we'd have a periscope so we'd know when the coast was clear on the surface. But if the periscope got BLOCKED, we might never know it was OK to go back UP.

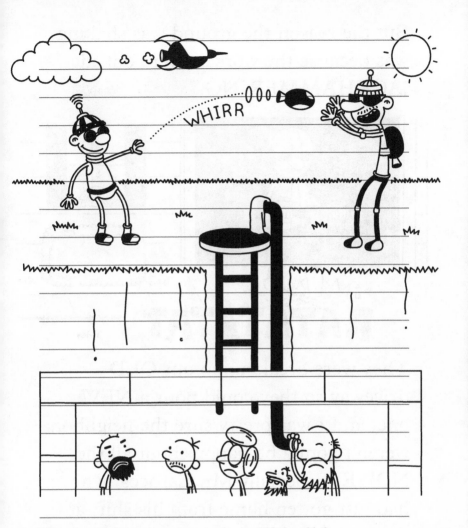

Dad said some people still build
bunkers so they can stay safe if there's
a natural disaster, like a TORNADO
or something. Well, this morning
I thought we were experiencing an
EARTHQUAKE, and the LAST place I
wanted to be was underground.

But the reason the ground was shaking was because the workers were outside JACKHAMMERING.

RATATATAT

They were breaking up our OLD driveway so they could pour a NEW one, and I was pretty sure the neighbors weren't gonna be happy about all the NOISE. Especially Mr. Larocca, who had just gotten home from his shift at the hospital.

RATAT ATATAT

But I was EXCITED about the new driveway. Our old one was in really bad shape, so you couldn't really USE it for anything. And maybe that's what's been holding me back from becoming a professional athlete all this time.

SLAM

When they hauled the rubble away and the truck came to pour the fresh concrete, I started to get NERVOUS.

A lot of the kids in my neighborhood are JERKS, and if they see wet concrete, they'll write stupid stuff in it.

On top of that, Mrs. Rutkowski's
CATS have been in our yard a lot lately
hunting for MICE, and I didn't want
a bunch of paw prints in the freshly
poured concrete.

So after the workers finished, I patrolled
the perimeter to make sure everyone
stayed OFF.

I was watching the STREET, but it
turns out I should've been watching the
GARAGE.

I heard the door open, and Rodrick started pulling his VAN out. I tried to STOP him, but he was playing his music too loud to hear.

I couldn't BELIEVE no one inside the house told Rodrick about the driveway. But it turns out they had a really good excuse, because they were dealing with a more SERIOUS problem.

SMOKE was pouring out of the windows on the first floor, and I heard SIRENS in the distance.

Mom came running out the front door, and Dad was right behind her.

Ten seconds later, a FIRE TRUCK pulled up along the curb, and a couple of firefighters got out.

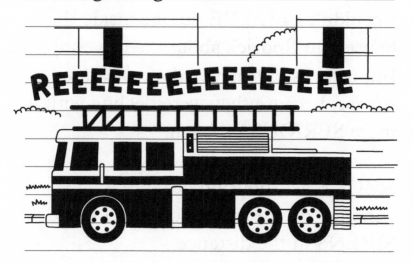

They ran across the lawn and onto the front walkway, which the workers had just finished pouring.

SPLISH   SPLOOSH

That's when everyone realized that MANNY was still inside. But thankfully he'd already had PRACTICE for this sort of thing.

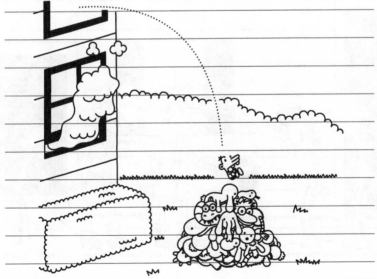

The GOOD news is, there wasn't actually a FIRE, there was just a lot of SMOKE. But the bad news is, it was MY fault.

Last week, when we were putting our food in places where the mice couldn't get it, I hid some snacks in the OVEN.

So when Mom preheated the oven to put in a batch of bacon this morning, a plastic bag MELTED. It's kind of UNFORTUNATE, because that was a waste of some perfectly good potato chips.

And this was definitely one of those times when I could've used that escape hatch in the back of my closet.

Wednesday
Believe it or not, Mom and Dad have already moved past the whole potato chip bag incident. And that's good news for ME.

But the REASON they've forgotten about it is the BAD news.

A few days ago, the building inspector came out to check the framing of the addition.

And when he DID, he found out the whole structure was too close to Mrs. Tuttle's property line by about three FEET.

I guess the construction company messed up when they created the plans for the addition, but the town didn't catch the mistake when they issued the building permit. So now there was just a bunch of finger-pointing, and no one would take any responsibility.

The building inspector told us the only thing we could really do NOW was to get our next-door neighbor to sign something that says we had permission to build the structure close to her property line. But that wasn't gonna be EASY.

The other day, when the concrete guys came back to patch up the driveway and front walk, they set up their cement mixer on our lawn. But I guess they forgot we were on a HILL, because the mixer tipped over and poured fresh concrete right into Mrs. Tuttle's GARDEN.

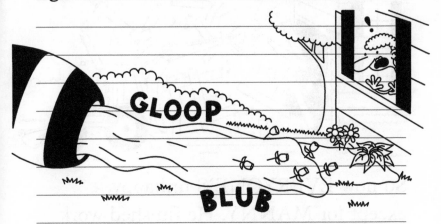

So when Mom and Dad asked for Mrs. Tuttle's permission to keep our addition where it WAS, she wasn't looking to do them any favors.

Mrs. Tuttle wouldn't BUDGE, and
the town told Mom and Dad the
whole structure was gonna have to
come DOWN. And that's exactly what
happened this afternoon.

So now EVERYONE'S unhappy,
except for MANNY. He finished work
on HIS place TODAY, and he had a
housewarming party to celebrate.

Thursday

Mom's been in a real funk ever since the addition was torn down.

I figured we'd just start over and build it the RIGHT way this time. But Mom said we burned through most of Aunt Reba's inheritance during construction, and we were gonna need to spend the REST patching up the side of the house.

So Mom was ALREADY in a bad mood when my test results came in the mail, and they didn't cheer her up any.

It wasn't only MY scores that were bad, though. The whole GRADE did poorly, and I can tell you the reason WHY.

During the middle of the test, some kid let the Stress Lizard out of its case, and it's really hard to CONCENTRATE when there's a REPTILE on the loose.

So I guess this means the school is gonna lose its funding, and Mom's not HAPPY about it.

In fact, she's so upset she's saying we should MOVE so we can live in a better school district.

But nobody ELSE is crazy about moving to another town. Dad grew up here, and he says he doesn't see any REASON to move.

And RODRICK doesn't wanna leave, either. He says his band is FAMOUS in our town, and he doesn't wanna start over somewhere else. But I don't know how famous you can really BE if your last concert was at a bowling alley.

Rodrick says he's NEVER moving, and even if the REST of us moved out, he'd just keep living in the basement.

And to be honest with you, I don't think Rodrick would even NOTICE if a new family moved in.

I don't think MANNY'S going anywhere, either. He just put in a sprinkler system, and his yard is really coming in nice.

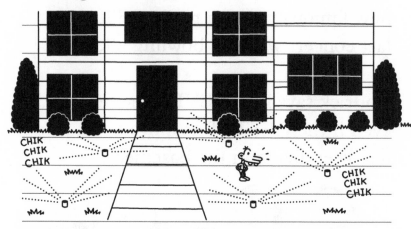

Truthfully, I didn't know how I felt about moving. I guess I'm OK with where we live now, but maybe it wouldn't be such a bad idea to start fresh somewhere ELSE.

The great thing about moving is that when you go to a new place, you can decide who you wanna BE.

Maybe I could come up with a new LOOK, and people would think I was a "bad boy."

I could even become a whole new PERSON, and tell everyone I'm a professional snowboarder or something.

But maybe I could take it even further than THAT. I could pretend I'm from another COUNTRY where they don't speak English.

And then my teachers would be impressed when I picked up some new phrases.

It's actually kind of FUN imagining a whole new life for myself in a different place.

Back in elementary school, we used to play this game called M.A.S.H., which stands for Mansion, Apartment, Shack, House. I'd write down all the possibilities for my future, and then roll a die over and over and scratch things off until I only had one item left in each category.

I actually found some of my old M.A.S.H. sheets from the fifth grade in my closet a few weeks back.

M.A.S.H.

Home	Location
~~Mansion~~	~~Mountain~~
(Apartment)	(Desert)
~~Shack~~	~~Jungle~~
~~House~~	~~Iceberg~~

Job	Salary
~~Doctor~~	~~$1,000,000~~
(Zookeeper)	~~$100,000~~
~~Plumber~~	($1,000)
~~Magician~~	~~$0~~

Wife	# Kids
~~Holly~~	~~0~~
~~Becky~~	(1)
(Erin)	~~4~~
~~None~~	~~20~~

167

Whenever I played, I always hoped I'd get a perfect result. But even if I got a good choice in most categories, there would always be that one item that ruined EVERYTHING.

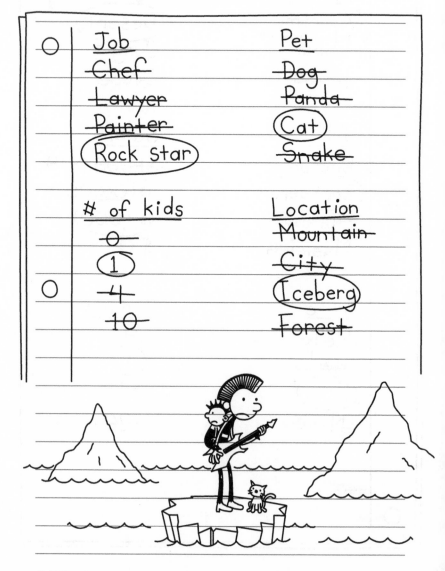

O
Job
~~Chef~~
~~Lawyer~~
~~Painter~~
(Rock star)

Pet
~~Dog~~
~~Panda~~
(Cat)
~~Snake~~

# of kids
~~0~~
(1)
~~4~~
~~10~~

O

Location
~~Mountain~~
~~City~~
(Iceberg)
~~Forest~~

One of the reasons I liked playing M.A.S.H. so much was because it was a good chance to hang out with the girls at recess. And the girl I liked the MOST back then was Becky Anton.

So sometimes I'd cheat a little when I was filling out my M.A.S.H. categories to guarantee I got a good result.

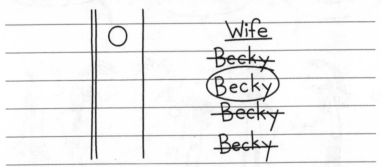

These days, Becky hardly knows who I AM, even though we're lab partners in Biology. I keep thinking I should bring up the fact that we're supposed to get MARRIED one day, but the timing never seems right.

That's ANOTHER good reason to move. I could SERIOUSLY improve my dating situation. Because if there's one thing girls love, it's the NEW guy.

Kelson Garrity was the new guy at the beginning of this school year. And when he showed up, the girls went CRAZY for him.

Well, it took a few weeks before everyone realized Kelson was kind of WEIRD, and now the girls won't go NEAR him. But he had a good run for a while there.

So there are probably a LOT of good reasons to move. In fact, the only DOWNSIDE is that I'd need to find a new BEST FRIEND.

And I don't know if that would be WORTH it. I've invested a lot of time and energy into Rowley, and I can't really see myself starting over with someone NEW.

But if we DO end up moving, I've got a whole list of REQUIREMENTS for a future best friend.

Number ONE, they've got to like to WATCH somebody playing video games more than they like playing games themselves.

Number TWO, it would be nice if they could actually DRAW. Because I'm really into creating comics and stuff.

And number THREE, they've gotta have junk cereal in their house. I don't know if I can be friends with another kid whose parents are health nuts.

But most important, they've gotta have a good sense of HUMOR. Because if there's one thing you should know about me, it's that I'm kind of a practical joker.

Saturday

So it turns out Mom is actually SERIOUS about this moving thing. She's been spending time each night looking at different houses online, and I'VE kind of gotten into it, TOO.

Every place we've looked at so far has some kind of ISSUE, though. There was one house with a big backyard, but it was right near a sewage treatment plant. And there was another one that was brand new, but the house only had one bathroom. Me and Mom were ready to give up looking, but then we found a place that looked PERFECT.

Your Dream Home

3,000 square foot home in desirable neighborhood. 4 bed, 2.5 bath colonial. Updates include gleaming hardwood floors and modern light fixtures.

The house is just a few years old, and
it looks like it's in a nice neighborhood.
But what got MOM most excited was
the big KITCHEN.

Mom looked up the school system, and
the test scores were pretty good. Then
she called the realtor to find out when
we could go SEE the place.

The realtor said there was an open
house this weekend, and we should drop
by if we could. So this morning, Mom
told everyone to get in the van to check
the place out.

Nobody else was HAPPY about that,
because like I said before, the rest of my
family doesn't want to MOVE.

But when we pulled into the neighborhood, everyone started to change their tune.

The realtor let our family in and showed us around the house, which was WAY nicer than ours. And the kitchen was even bigger than it looked in the PICTURES.

But what really got my attention was the
SWIMMING POOL in the backyard.

Rodrick and Manny must've spotted it
before I did, because both of them were
already out there by the time I got down
the back stairs.

We've been trying to get Mom and Dad to put a pool in our backyard FOREVER. They always tell us that the hot tub is just as GOOD as a pool, but believe me, it's not the same.

And this was an IN-GROUND pool. We actually had an aboveground pool when I was younger, but it didn't even last a WEEK.

BLOOSH

The realtor showed us a few more features of the house, but she didn't NEED to because we were already SOLD.

On our way home, everyone was super excited. Rodrick said he's gonna use the pool to do summer CONCERTS, and it'll be a totally crazy scene every Friday night.

I decided I'm gonna CHARGE people to come use our pool, but that I'll make exceptions for CERTAIN people.

But Manny was the most excited of ALL. He's got big plans for the pool, too, and all I can say is, it's gonna take a lot of chocolate PUDDING.

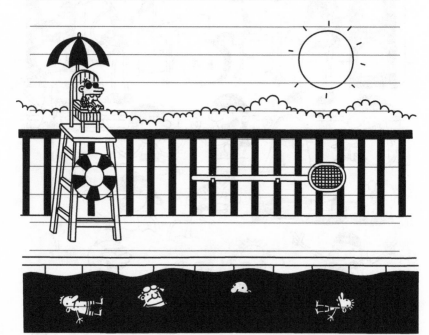

Monday

We had another family meeting
last night, and this was a BIG one.
Everyone's on board with moving to the
new house, so that's great.

Mom told us not to TELL anyone yet,
because we still have to sell OUR house
so we can afford to buy the NEW one.
It was a little hard for me to keep that
information to MYSELF, though, and
I figured there wouldn't be any harm in
telling just ONE person.

But maybe I should've told someone
besides ROWLEY, because he didn't
take the news too well.

I guess I could've eased Rowley into it instead of hitting him with the information all at once.

I tried to make him feel better by saying we'd stay FRIENDS and that he could come use my pool on days when it wasn't too CROWDED. But that didn't seem to cheer him up at ALL.

Hopefully Rowley will come around, though, because I'm not sure I can deal with this kind of drama every day.

After dinner tonight, Mom asked her friend who's a realtor to come over and help us sell OUR house. So we went from room to room, and Mrs. Laghari told us what we were gonna have to CHANGE before we could put it on the market.

She said we were gonna need to replace our carpets, give everything a fresh coat of paint, and put new tile in the kitchen and bathrooms. And that was just for STARTERS.

Mrs. Laghari said that we'd have to take down our family photos, because buyers like to imagine THEMSELVES living in the house. Well, that was fine with ME, because there are SOME pictures that should've come down a long TIME ago.

Then Mrs. Laghari told us that when we have an open house, we should lock the basement door so no one sees what's down there.

The last thing Mrs. Laghari told us is that most of our furniture is "outdated," and we should probably just cover it up with sheets for the open house. I think that hurt Mom's feelings, and she said people would LOVE her taste in furniture.

But Mrs. Laghari said that if we didn't do all the things she recommended, she'd have a hard time selling our house. So Mom said in THAT case we'd sell the house OURSELVES, and she showed Mrs. Laghari to the door.

I guess this means Mom and Mrs. Laghari aren't FRIENDS anymore. But that's OK, because we're moving soon ANYWAY.

Sunday
Mom wants to prove our house is great the way it IS, so we're trying to sell it without making any big changes. The open house was this afternoon, but we spent the whole WEEK getting ready for it.

It was MY job to write the description to post online. And I got a little creative to try and make it stand out.

> **Four-bedroom house with three bathrooms in nice neighborhood. Home of former bank robber. Possible gold/rare coins buried under floorboards.**

We took photos of every room and posted those, too. The house was a MESS when we took the pictures, though, so we had to move some stuff around to make it LOOK clean.

FLASH

The open house started at noon, and we really had to scramble to get everything nice and neat. We did the best we could and got out of there just before people started to arrive.

But it was kind of hard sitting there doing NOTHING while total strangers were going into our house.

Mom said none of the people at our open house actually knew we were the OWNERS, so WE could pretend to be checking the place out, TOO. And that way we could listen in on what everyone was saying.

Well, I thought that sounded kind of FUN, so I went inside with Mom. But everyone ELSE in the family thought it was a dumb idea and stayed back in the van.

It turns out the spying idea was a MISTAKE, though. Most of the people didn't have anything NICE to say about our house, and it was kind of tough hearing all the criticism.

THE CEILINGS ARE SO LOW!

AND THESE CABINETS ARE IN TERRIBLE SHAPE!

But I think Mom was taking it a little harder than I was. Because whenever someone had something NEGATIVE to say, she'd speak up.

Mom got so upset that she went back out to the van. But I stayed in the HOUSE, because I wasn't comfortable with all these random strangers poking around our things.

But not everyone was exploring the house. There were a bunch of men in the family room watching a football game, and from the look of things, they had helped themselves to our SNACKS.

These guys were letting their kids run wild in our house while they kicked back and watched TV. So they were basically using the open house for free BABYSITTING.

Since these dads weren't watching their KIDS, it was up to ME to make sure they didn't BREAK anything.

But I couldn't be everywhere at ONCE, and I was upstairs chasing kids out of our bathroom when there was a loud noise DOWNSTAIRS.

CRASH

It sounded like a kid tipped over the FRIDGE or something, so I ran down to make sure nobody was HURT. But it wasn't a KID who made the noise, it was one of the DADS.

One of the guys went into the laundry room looking for more SNACKS, but that's where we were keeping all the stuff we couldn't hide anywhere ELSE.

I guess the noise freaked out the other dads, because they scooped up their kids and left in a HURRY.

So that was the end of the open house, and we didn't get a SINGLE offer.

At dinner tonight, everyone was kind of bummed out. But while we were doing the dishes, there was a knock on the front door.

It was a couple from out of town, and they said they couldn't make it to the open house in time. So Mom invited them in to show them around.They seemed pretty IMPRESSED, and the lady said EXACTLY what Mom wanted to hear.

I JUST LOVE YOUR TASTE IN FURNITURE!

And believe it or not, they made an offer right on the spot.

<u>Saturday</u>

I knew I was gonna have to tell Rowley we were selling our house, but I didn't want a repeat of what happened the LAST time we talked about it.

I came up with an idea for how to handle it THIS time around. There's a Preston Platypus book on this EXACT subject, and I figured it was the PERFECT way to get Rowley used to the idea of me moving. So I brought the book with me to his house this afternoon.

It felt a little AWKWARD reading a story to Rowley. But I think he's USED to having books read to him, so he made himself comfortable.

I don't really think the message of the book was getting THROUGH to Rowley, though. And the story kind of made me MAD, anyway. It was about how Preston Platypus has a best friend named Pelican Pete, and they do EVERYTHING together.

But then one day Pelican Pete says he's MOVING, and Preston Platypus is sad. And I was FINE with the story up to that point.

Then Preston's mom tells him he'll make NEW friends after Pete moves, and everything will work out for the best. Sure enough, by the end of the book, that's EXACTLY what happens.

And so Preston and his NEW pals had fun all summer long.

THE END

So basically Preston Platypus forgets about Pelican Pete, and all their years of friendship don't mean a THING. And we never find out what happens to Pelican Pete or if he's happy in HIS new neighborhood.

196

I thought about writing an angry letter to whoever WROTE this garbage. But of course Rowley LIKED the story, and he wanted me to read him ANOTHER one.

I decided to just stop dancing around the issue and tell Rowley what was REALLY going on. And the second I did, I REGRETTED it.

I told Rowley to try not to get too worked up because it wasn't a done deal yet. But nothing I said made any difference.

I had to tell Rowley that if he was gonna be so DRAMATIC, I was going HOME.

So then Rowley promised he'd keep himself together, and he DID, but just BARELY.

Maybe it was a mistake telling Rowley about ANY of this. I probably should've sent him a postcard AFTER I moved, because that would've been a lot easier on BOTH of us.

Wednesday
The owners of the house with the pool accepted our offer, so I guess this is really HAPPENING.

The people who are buying OUR place did a home inspection over the weekend, and they found a few things we're gonna have to fix before they'll buy the house. The most SERIOUS issue was a problem with the ceiling underneath Mom and Dad's shower.

Apparently that clogged drain was a bigger problem than we THOUGHT. The floorboards under the bathroom tile were totally rotted out, so now we're gonna have to REPLACE them.

We're lucky nothing TERRIBLE ever happened. Because I can think of things even worse than the GROUT.

The other thing the buyers want us to do is get rid of the HOT TUB, because they have young kids and they're worried about SAFETY. And I'm 100% with them on THAT one.

Now that I know for SURE we're moving, I have a TOTALLY different attitude about school. Since it's almost summer, I asked Mom if I could SKIP classes for the rest of the year.

But she said if I don't go to school, they could throw her and Dad in JAIL. I thought about whether or not that would be WORTH it, but I decided I could just suck it up for a little while longer.

I realized that next year I won't be going to school with these kids, and that's what gave me the courage to finally tell Becky Anton that I LIKED her. So during Biology I told Becky I'd had a crush on her ever since fifth grade.

But Becky went straight to the TEACHER, and five minutes later I had a new lab partner. And I'm seriously thinking about the JAIL option again, because I don't know if I can last the rest of the school year dealing with Kelson Garrity.

DIG DIG

That's not even my WORST problem, though. Ever since I told Rowley that we're officially MOVING, he's been a total MESS. Even though he keeps promising he's not gonna go all BLUBBERY on me, the smallest thing can set him off.

And even when he IS keeping it together, he still says these little things that make me feel GUILTY about moving.

I GUESS THIS IS THE LAST TIME WE'LL EVER EAT GRILLED CHEESE SANDWICHES TOGETHER!

On the way home from school today, we had to walk in the grass because they'd just repaved the sidewalk. But that gave Rowley an IDEA. He said we should write our NAMES in the cement with a stick and put "BEST FRIENDS" underneath.

It made me a little uncomfortable writing in something so PERMANENT, though, especially since I didn't know what the friend situation would be in my new neighborhood. I didn't wanna mention that to Rowley, because I knew it would set him off again.

So I wrote some extra stuff with the stick to give me a little wiggle room, just in case.

Greg & Rowley
BEST
FRIENDS*

* currently

Saturday
School ended a week ago, and while everyone ELSE is already enjoying their summer vacation, we've been PACKING.

TOSS

Mom created a binder and a schedule for everyone in the family, and we're all responsible for boxing up our own stuff. It's gonna be TIGHT, but we should be done by the time the moving trucks show up next weekend.

The person who's taking the LONGEST is DAD. He wants to make sure none of his Civil War figurines break, so he's using a whole roll of bubble wrap for each ONE.

Mom's been hoping our neighbors would throw us a going-away party, but with all the construction over the past month, we're not that POPULAR around here. So Mom decided we'd just throw a party for OURSELVES.

The party was TONIGHT. We'd sent out invitations to just about everyone on our street, and we set everything up in our yard.

Rodrick was excited, because Mom and Dad were letting his band play, and they were even PAYING him. We were still busy setting up when the first guests started to arrive.

I wasn't sure if I should even INVITE Rowley to the party, because I was afraid he might have another breakdown. But I was actually really happy to see him.

His parents seemed happy, TOO, and I almost got the feeling they were GLAD I was moving.

Rowley said he had a GIFT for me, which was a giant collage with a bunch of pictures of us over the years. And I'm not gonna lie, it got me a little choked up.

I was kind of RELIEVED that's all
Rowley's gift was. Because the way
he's been acting lately, I wouldn't be
surprised if he gave me one of his
FINGERS or something.

Rowley said I could hang the collage
in my NEW bedroom to remind me of
all the fun stuff we did together. And I
don't know if there was a lot of pollen in
the air tonight or WHAT, but right then
I think I got something in my eye.

Things were getting a little too touchy-
feely for me, though, so I was glad when
more people started to arrive at the party.

It picked up really FAST from there. Rodrick's band started playing out on the back deck, and the music attracted some teenagers who were at a high school graduation party a few doors down. Then it seemed like everyone on our street was at our party all at ONCE, and it got CRAZY.

Our party was pretty WILD, but it was NOTHING compared to MANNY'S. And his party was still going strong when I turned in for the night.

Sunday
I have to admit, last night was a lot of FUN. But I'm kind of SAD, because just when things are getting GOOD around here, we're LEAVING.

I was the first one in the house awake today, and when I looked out the window, I knew we were in for a long day of cleanup.

I wished we still had that DUMPSTER, because that would've made things a whole lot EASIER.

While I was looking over the front lawn, two big moving trucks pulled up along the curb. I was kind of CONFUSED, because our move was still a week away.

A few guys got out of the trucks, and one of them came to our front door. So I went out to MEET him.

The man told me his team was ready to start putting our stuff into the trucks, and they needed to come inside the house. By now, Mom had come downstairs and was at the front door.

She told the guy he was a week EARLY, and that the move wasn't until NEXT Sunday. But he pulled out a contract that showed TODAY'S date as the moving day, and it had Mom's SIGNATURE on the bottom.

Mom told the guy she made a MISTAKE, and that we weren't READY to move yet. He told her the deposit was "nonrefundable," and that if we didn't move TODAY, we'd lose the money we already paid.

Now Mom was in a PANIC. She woke everyone up and told us to get PACKING. The movers said we had a two-hour window to get everything onto the trucks, so we really had to HUSTLE.

Up to this point we'd been really careful packing so nothing got DAMAGED. But now there was no TIME for that.

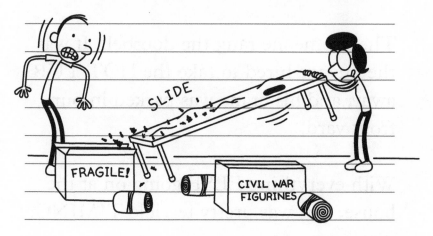

The movers REALLY didn't care if our stuff got broken. And that's why it was probably a bad idea to let them pack up our DISHES.

Mom asked the movers to just focus on the FURNITURE instead, and they went down to the basement to start there.

Then someone rang the doorbell. It was the guy we hired to take the HOT TUB away, and his crane was parked in our front yard.

With everything ELSE going on at the house, this was pretty terrible TIMING.

The crane operator explained that he couldn't get his vehicle into our backyard without running over our neighbor's flower garden, so his plan was to lift the hot tub OVER the house.

That sounded a little crazy to ME, but I figured this guy probably knew what he was doing.

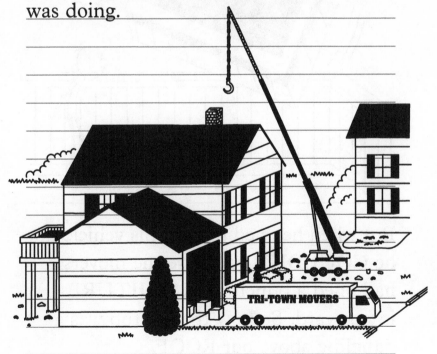

TRI-TOWN MOVERS

I showed the guy where the hot tub was, and he put some straps around it. Then he attached the straps to a giant HOOK and lifted the hot tub off the deck.

But when he tried to back his vehicle up, he COULDN'T, because the movers had piled a bunch of FURNITURE in our yard. So now the hot tub was dangling above our ROOF.

216

As if the whole situation wasn't stressful enough ALREADY, all of a sudden ROWLEY showed up in my front yard.

But I didn't have TIME to deal with Rowley, because now I had a NEW problem.

That guy from Whirley Street had pulled up in front of our house, and he was taking the FURNITURE that the movers had left by the curb. And that's when I remembered it was SUNDAY, which is the day we leave our TRASH out.

DUMP

I tried to wave the guy off to make him go away. But the crane operator thought I was giving him a signal that it was OK to back up his vehicle, which is what he DID.

And that was the end of our living room COUCH.

The CRANE stopped, but the hot tub DIDN'T. It started swinging in crazy circles above the house, and then it slammed into our CHIMNEY.

The bricks slid off the roof and just missed my PARENTS, who had come outside to see what all the COMMOTION was.

After that, I thought it was OVER, because I couldn't imagine anything ELSE happening. But something DID.

Some wasps had built a nest in our CHIMNEY, which explains how they were getting into the house all this time. And now they were LOOSE, looking for REVENGE.

We all ran for cover inside the house, but the crane operator wasn't quick enough to get away.

The wasps flew in the cabin of his vehicle, which made him kick the lever that released the HOT TUB, which fell through the ROOF.

And at that point, to tell the truth, I was kind of RELIEVED. Because now I knew for SURE that things really couldn't get any WORSE.

Thursday

There was one bright spot from what happened over the weekend, and it's that Rodrick made it through the experience ALIVE.

The hot tub landed smack in the middle of his BEDROOM, so we thought he got CRUSHED. But when the movers had hauled Rodrick's bed out of the basement, they loaded it onto one of the trucks and took him WITH it.

Everything else is BAD news. The people who were supposed to buy OUR house pulled out, and that meant we couldn't afford the NEW one. So I guess that means we're STUCK here for a while.

To be honest with you, I'm not totally sure I was ready to move, anyway. Looking for a new best friend would've been a huge hassle, and besides, there's so much more I need to TEACH Rowley before I go.

There's probably a LESSON I could learn from this whole experience, like "be happy with what you've got" or "there's no place like home" or that sort of thing. But that's the kind of corny stuff they put in books for little kids.

So here's the lesson I'M taking away from all this: Don't be late for an old lady's funeral. Because believe me, she'll make you PAY.

ACKNOWLEDGMENTS

Thanks to my wife, Julie, for your love and support, especially during my deadlines. Thanks to my family for cheering me on all these years.

Thanks to Charlie Kochman for caring about every period, comma, and semicolon in these books. Thanks to everyone at Abrams, including Michael Jacobs, Andrew Smith, Hallie Patterson, Melanie Chang, Kim Lauber, Mary O'Mara, Alison Gervais, and Elisa Gonzalez. Thanks also to Susan Van Metre and Steve Roman.

Thanks to my awesome, friendly Wimpy Kid team: Shaelyn Germain, Anna Cesary, and Vanessa Jedrej. Thanks to Deb Sundin, Kym Havens, and the incredible staff at An Unlikely Story.

Special thanks to Chad W. Beckerman for your outstanding design skills and for your friendship over these many years. Thanks to Liz Fithian for all the great memories on our travels.

Thanks to Rich Carr and Andrea Lucey for your outstanding support. Thanks to Paul Sennott for all your help. Thanks to Sylvie Rabineau and Keith Fleer for everything you do for me.

As always, thanks to Jess Brallier for your continued support.

ABOUT THE AUTHOR

Jeff Kinney is a #1 *New York Times* best-selling author and a six-time Nickelodeon Kids' Choice Award winner for Favorite Book. Jeff has been named one of *Time* magazine's 100 Most Influential People in the World. He is also the creator of Poptropica, which was named one of *Time*'s 50 Best Websites. He spent his childhood in the Washington, D.C., area and moved to New England in 1995. Jeff lives with his wife and two sons in Massachusetts, where they own a bookstore, An Unlikely Story.

The employees of Thorndike Press hope you have enjoyed this Large Print book. All our Thorndike, Wheeler, and Kennebec Large Print titles are designed for easy reading, and all our books are made to last. Other Thorndike Press Large Print books are available at your library, through selected bookstores, or directly from us.

For information about titles, please call:
    (800) 223-1244

or visit our website at:
    http://gale.cengage.com/thorndike

To share your comments, please write:
    Publisher
    Thorndike Press
    10 Water St., Suite 310
    Waterville, ME 04901